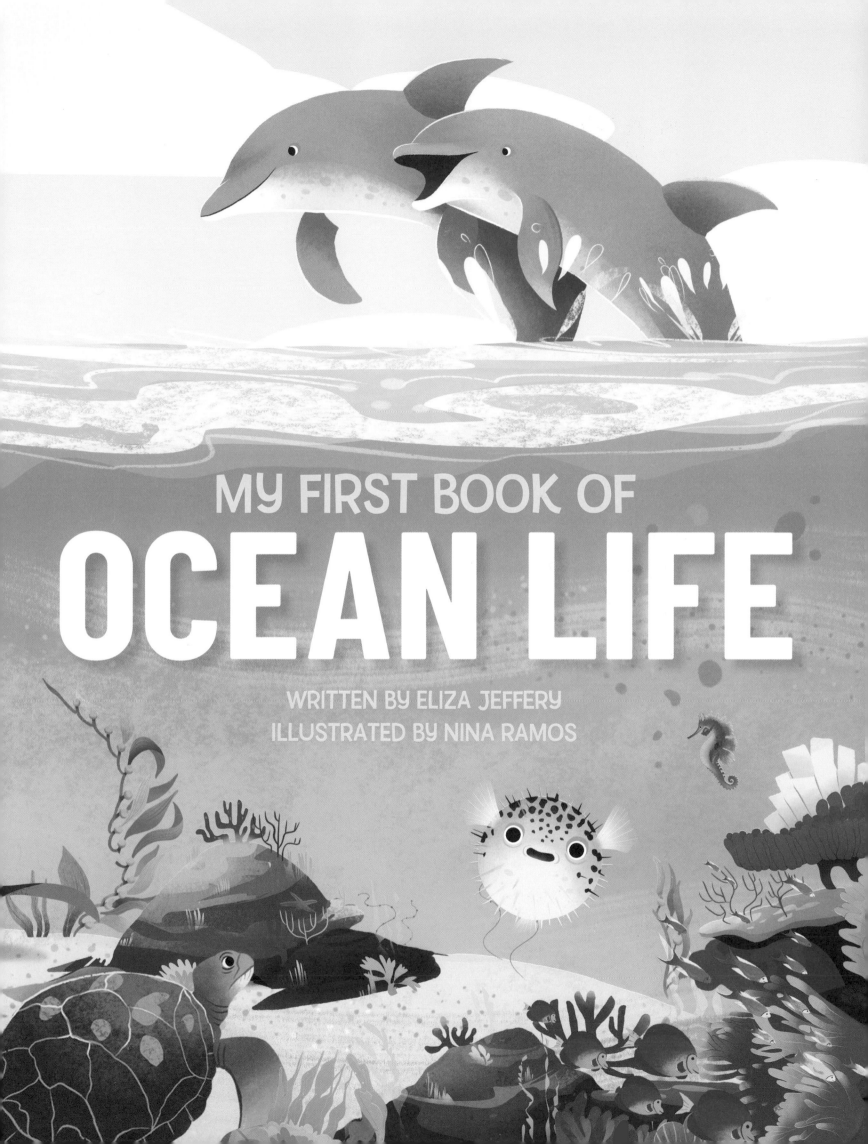

MY FIRST BOOK OF
OCEAN LIFE

WRITTEN BY ELIZA JEFFERY

ILLUSTRATED BY NINA RAMOS

CONTENTS

Ocean Life	8
Whales	10
Coral	12
Crab	14
Jellyfish	16
Dolphin	18
Octopus	20
Sea Turtle	22
Sharks	24
Penguin	26
Sea Otter	28
Rays	30
Pufferfish	32
Seahorse	34
Starfish	36
Seal	38
Keeping Oceans Healthy	40
The Big Blue	42
Index	44
Glossary	45

Words in BOLD can be found in the glossary.

OCEAN LIFE

The ocean is MASSIVE!

The ocean covers most of our planet. It is home to some wonderful creatures of all shapes and sizes. The oceans are important for helping all animals to survive. There are five different oceans around the world:

ATLANTIC OCEAN

The second-largest ocean in the world. There are lots of interesting **species** in the Atlantic Ocean, including sea turtles and dolphins.

PACIFIC OCEAN

The largest and deepest ocean in the world. The Pacific Ocean is home to the Great Barrier Reef, which is the largest coral reef in the world!

ANTARCTIC OCEAN

The most recently named ocean in the world. The Antarctic Ocean has 17 different penguin species.

ARCTIC OCEAN

The smallest ocean in the world.
The Arctic Ocean has a variety of
species, from polar bears to whales!

INDIAN OCEAN

The Indian Ocean covers
a large area of the world's
surface. Lots of marine animals
swim in these waters, including
rays and sea turtles.

WHALES

Whales are the BIGGEST MAMMALS in the world!

Whales communicate with each other using songs and clicks, which can travel long distances underwater. They have a thick layer of blubber for warmth.

All whales have a tail and fins.

Killer whales are actually a type of dolphin!

The blue whale is the largest animal that's ever lived!

DID YOU KNOW?

I eat... lots of things, from tiny plankton to large **mammals** like sea lions.

I am found in... deep and shallow water.

I live in a group called... a pod.

My babies are called... calves.

Whales have a blowhole for breathing.

11

CORAL

coral has been on Earth for 240 MILLION YEARS!

Coral may look like pretty rocks and plants but it is actually an animal! It stays in one place during its lifetime and becomes a home for lots of other sea creatures. When coral grows together, it's called a coral reef.

Tentacles to catch its food

DID YOU KNOW?

I eat... zooplankton.

I can be found in... deep and shallow water.

I live in a group called... a colony.

My babies are called... planulae (plan-you-lay).

Some coral can live for up to 5,000 years!

Coral is home to all sorts of ocean life.

13

CRAB

crabs talk to each other by rubbing their PINCERS together!

Crabs have exoskeletons, meaning their skeleton is on the outside of their bodies. They have ten legs, two pincers and an egg-shaped shell that protects them from **predators**.

Crabs walk and swim sideways.

Lobsters and crabs are part of the same family.

Crabs have flat bodies for fitting into small gaps

DID YOU KNOW?

I eat... seaweed, clams and small fish.

I can be found in... rockpools and oceans, although some prefer **freshwater habitats!**

I live in a group called... a cast.

My babies are called... zoea (zo-ee-uh).

Sharp pincers for catching food

JELLYFISH

Some jellyfish can GLOW IN THE DARK!

They have bag-like bodies and tentacles that can sting other animals. Jellyfish have no eyes, heart, bones or brain! They are **transparent**, meaning you can see through them.

Jellyfish are mostly made of water.

A jellyfish sting can be painful for humans!

Jellyfish can be pink, yellow, blue or purple!

DID YOU KNOW?

I eat... plankton, plants and small fish.

I can be found in... deep and shallow water.

I live in a group called... a smack.

My babies are called... ephyras (eh-fear-as).

DOLPHIN

Dolphins are one of the SMARTEST animals!

Dolphins are very social and playful creatures. They work together in groups to catch their **prey**. A dolphin can swim really fast, thanks to its narrow body and fins that help it to **steer**.

Dolphins need to come up to the surface to breathe.

DID YOU KNOW?

I eat... fish, squid and jellyfish.

I can be found in... shallow water.

I live in a group called... a pod.

My babies are called... calves.

They communicate through special whistles and clicks.

Smooth, rubbery skin

19

OCTOPUS

An octopus has EIGHT LEGS and NINE BRAINS!

They have no bones, which means they can squeeze into tight spaces. Octopuses can squirt ink to scare away predators that try to eat them, like whales and sea otters!

Octopuses have three hearts!

DID YOU KNOW?

I eat... crabs, snails and clams.

I can be found in... **coastal** areas.

I live in a group called... a consortium.

My babies are called... fry.

Tentacles with sticky suckers for catching food

They use **camouflage** to hide from predators.

SEA TURTLE

Sea turtles have been around since the DINOSAURS!

Female turtles come ashore to lay eggs on the beach. As soon as the eggs have hatched, the young make their own way to the water without any help!

Sea turtles can put their heads into their own shells!

DID YOU KNOW?

I eat... seagrass, algae and crabs.

I can be found in... shallow water.

I live in a group called... a bale.

My babies are called... hatchlings.

Sea turtles can hold their breath for 5 hours underwater!

Hard shells protect them from predators.

23

SHARKS

Sharks are FAST SWIMMERS!

They have an excellent sense of smell that helps them hunt prey, even when it's really far away. They have no bones in their body but plenty of teeth!

Hammerhead sharks have flat heads so they can feed on flat prey, like stingrays!

Sharp teeth for catching and eating prey

Sharks are at the top of the ocean **food chain**.

Powerful tails to swim quickly and smoothly through water

DID YOU KNOW?

I eat... seals, fish and sea lions.

I can be found in... deep oceans and coastal areas.

I live in a group called... a shiver.

My babies are called... pups.

25

PENGUIN

Penguins can survive in VERY COLD places!

These birds can't fly, but they are very strong swimmers. They can hold their breath for up to 20 minutes when diving underwater for fish.

Male penguins look after the eggs.

Flippers and **webbed feet** help them push themselves through the water.

Penguins huddle together for warmth.

DID YOU KNOW?

I eat... krill, squid and fish.

I can be found in... coastal areas and frozen water.

I live in a group called... a huddle.

My babies are called... chicks.

SEA OTTER

Sea otters have the THICKEST FUR of all animals!

They mostly live around seaweed to stop them from floating out to sea. They are known for being very playful! A sea otter can live its whole life without ever coming out of the water.

Otters cuddle their babies and nap when they're floating.

DID YOU KNOW?

I eat... fish and shellfish, like crabs.

I can be found in... coastal areas.

I live in a group called... a raft.

My babies are called... pups.

28

Otters bash shellfish with rocks to open them!

They wash themselves after eating to keep their fur clean.

RAYS

Rays are very CLEVER HUNTERS!

They use electrical signals to hunt their prey. Unlike most fish, rays have teeth to help them crush shellfish. They have no bones in their bodies.

Long tails to whip predators with!

Large fins to push themselves through the water

DID YOU KNOW?

I eat... shellfish and worms.

I can be found in...shallow water.

I live in a group called... a school.

My babies are called... pups.

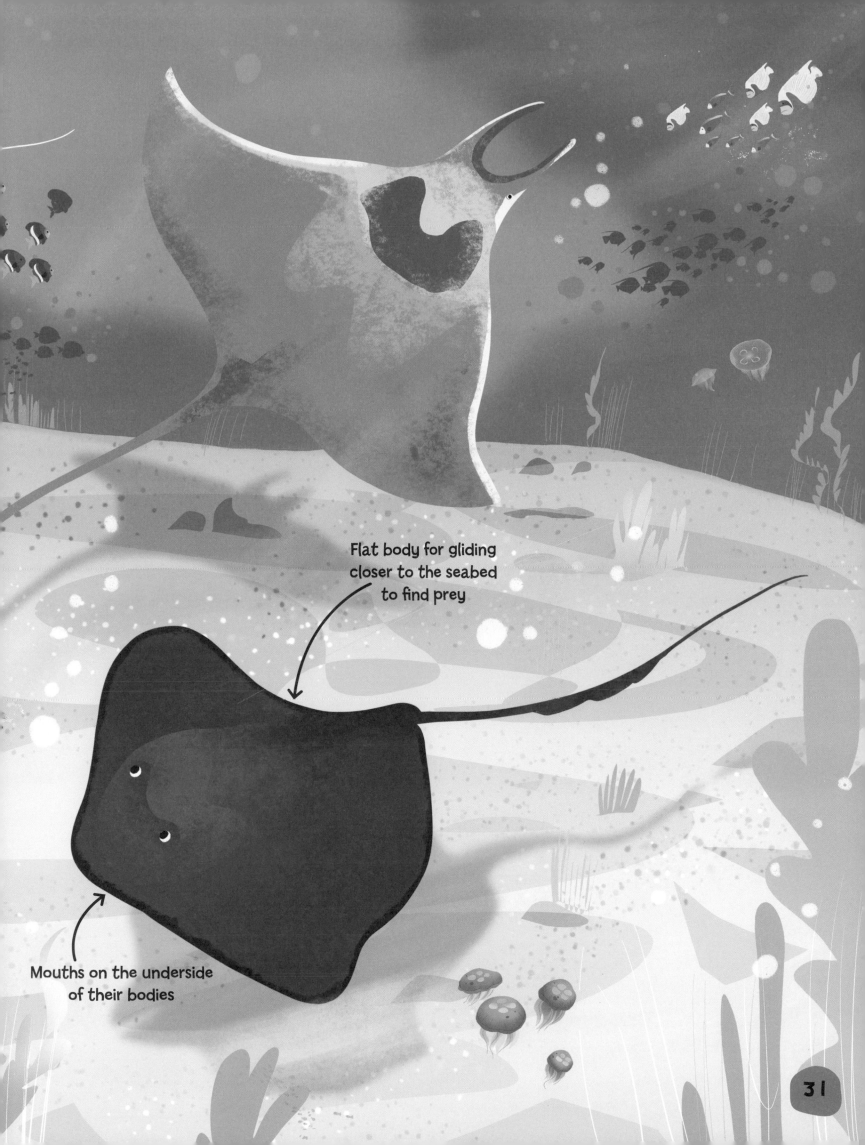

Flat body for gliding
closer to the seabed
to find prey

Mouths on the underside
of their bodies

PUFFERFISH
Pufferfish can inflate just like a BALLOON!

Pufferfish are poisonous, making them deadly for predators, like sharks. They can also hide in their surroundings by becoming darker or lighter.

Sharp spikes to keep predators away

Rough skin instead of scales

Their teeth never stop growing!

DID YOU KNOW?

I eat... algae, clams and mussels.

I can be found in... shallow water.

I live in a group called... a prickle.

My babies are called... fry.

SEAHORSE

Seahorses are a cross between HORSES AND MERMAIDS!

Seahorses don't have stomachs or teeth, so they suck their prey in through their snouts. They can make their bodies black, brown or yellow to hide from predators.

Seahorses use their tails to hold onto things, sometimes each other!

Male seahorses carry babies in a **brood pouch.**

Hard bodies make it difficult for predators to eat them

DID YOU KNOW?

I eat... plankton, shrimp and small fish.

I can be found in... warm, shallow water.

I live in a group called... a herd.

My babies are called... fry.

STARFISH

starfish can REGROW their arms!

They have no brain and move very slowly in the water.
A starfish eats by pushing its stomach out of its body!

They're not actually fish!

Hundreds of little feet help them to crawl.

Some starfish can grow up to 50 arms!

They come in lots of different shapes and sizes.

DID YOU KNOW?

I eat... clams, mussels and oysters.

I can be found in... deep and shallow water.

I live in a group called... a galaxy.

My babies are called... larvae.

SEAL
Seals can SLEEP UNDERWATER!

Seals are very playful creatures and live in groups.
A mother seal knows her baby just by its smell!

Thick layer of blubber for warmth

Seals can hold their breath underwater for up to 2 hours!

Flippers help them to swim and catch fish easily.

Some pups are born with fur!

DID YOU KNOW?

I eat... all kinds of fish!

I can be found in... coastal and open water.

I live in a group called... a herd.

My babies are called... pups.

KEEPING OCEANS HEALTHY

Our oceans are VERY IMPORTANT!

The oceans face many difficulties, but there are ways we can help prevent these problems and take care of our oceans.

CARING CORAL

You can save water in lots of ways, like turning off the tap while you brush your teeth! This keeps the oceans at the correct levels, allowing coral reefs to thrive.

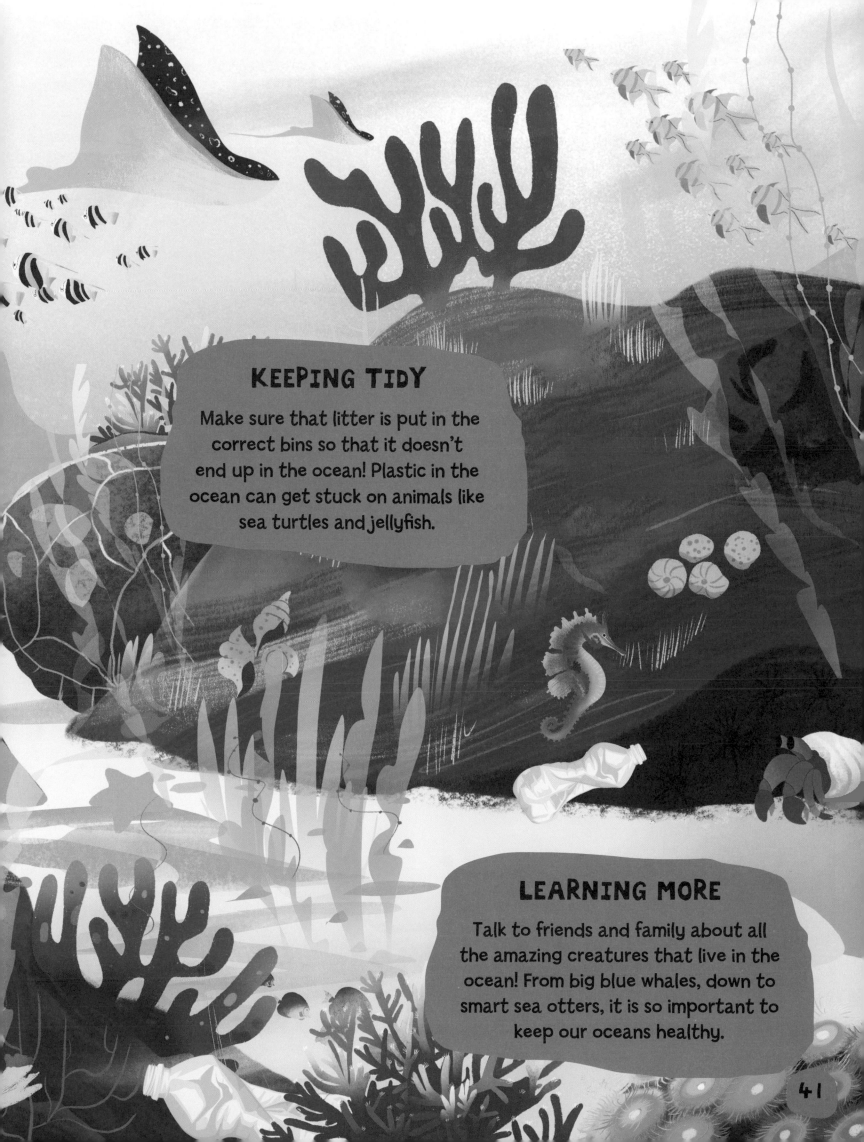

KEEPING TIDY

Make sure that litter is put in the correct bins so that it doesn't end up in the ocean! Plastic in the ocean can get stuck on animals like sea turtles and jellyfish.

LEARNING MORE

Talk to friends and family about all the amazing creatures that live in the ocean! From big blue whales, down to smart sea otters, it is so important to keep our oceans healthy.

THE BIG BLUE

The ocean is a big place! Now that we've explored some of the animals that live there, let's take a closer look at where in the ocean they can be found...

OPEN AND COASTAL WATERS

Can you spot anything on the shore? Animals like seals and crabs live on the edge of our oceans.

SHALLOW WATERS

Look out to sea! And what do you see? Marine creatures such as dolphins and turtles can be found here.

DEEP WATERS

It's very dark down here! Brave whales and sharks explore these deep waters.

43

INDEX

A
Antarctic Ocean 8-9
Arctic Ocean 8-9
Atlantic Ocean 8-9

C
coral 8, 12-13, 40
crab 14-15, 42

D
dolphin 8, 18-19, 42

I
Indian Ocean 8-9

J
jellyfish 16-17, 41

O
octopus 20-21

P
Pacific Ocean 8-9
penguin 8, 26-27
pufferfish 32-33

R
rays 9, 30-31

S
seahorse 34-35
seal 38-39, 42
sea otter 28-29, 41
sea turtle 8-9, 22-23, 41, 42
sharks 24-25, 43
starfish 36-37

W
whales 9, 10-11, 41, 43

First published in 2024 by Hungry Tomato Ltd.
F15, Old Bakery Studios, Blewetts Wharf,
Malpas Road, Truro, Cornwall, TR1 1QH, UK.

Thanks to our creative team:
Editor: Millie Burdett
Editor: Holly Thornton
Senior Designer: Amy Harvey

Copyright © 2024 Hungry Tomato Ltd

Beetle Books is an imprint of Hungry Tomato.

A CIP catalog record for this book is available
from the British Library.

ISBN: 9781916598607

Printed and bound in China

Discover more at
www.hungrytomato.com
www.mybeetlebooks.com

GLOSSARY

Brood pouch - a place where baby animals grow.

Camouflage - something that blends in with its surroundings so that it's difficult to see.

Coastal - an area of sea or ocean that is close to land.

Food chain - a way of showing how each animal gets its food.

Freshwater habitats - places with natural water that doesn't contain salt. It is found in rivers, ponds and lakes, but not in oceans.

Mammals - warm-blooded animals that give birth to live young and feed their babies with milk.

Predators - animals that hunt and kill other animals for food.

Prey - animals which are hunted by other animals as food.

Species - a group of living things that are the same as each other. For example, hammerhead shark and great white shark are different species.

Steer (verb) - to control direction.

Transparent - something that you can see clearly through.

Webbed feet - toes that are connected by a thin piece of skin. Some animals have these to help them swim.